The Children's Illustrated
ACTIVITY ATLAS

NEIL MORRIS

Gareth Stevens Children's Books
MILWAUKEE

For a free color catalog describing Gareth Stevens' list of high-quality children's books call 1 (800) 433-0942

Library of Congress Cataloging-in-Publication Data
Morris, Neil.
  The children's illustrated activity atlas.

  Includes index.
  Summary: Maps, activities, and text introduce regions and countries of the world and provide the opportunity to practice the reading of maps and the interpretation of atlas symbols.
  1. Atlases. [1. Atlases. 2. Maps] I. Title. II. Title: Activity atlas.
G1021.M67   1989   912   88-42913
ISBN 1-55532-927-6

North American edition first published in 1989 by
Gareth Stevens Children's Books
7317 West Green Tree Road
Milwaukee, Wisconsin 53223, USA

Project editor: Neil Champion
Editor (US): Mark Sachner
Research editor (US): Scott Enk

Printed in the United States of America
1 2 3 4 5 6 7 8 9 95 94 93 92 91 90 89

CONTENTS

What is a map?

A map is an accurately drawn picture of the things around us on the Earth's surface. Maps are very useful because they show you the shape of the land, help you find out how far it is from one place to another, and show you how to get there.

Some maps only show a very small part of Earth. This may be your school or the city or village where you live. Other maps show entire regions, countries, or continents.

A globe shows Earth's shape as it really is. But a map must change this round shape so we can flatten it out.

Maps show water and dry land, high mountains and low plains, on sheets of flat paper. It is not very easy to do this. A whole town, country, or even the world must fit onto a sheet of paper. This is done by using scale (see page 8).

The world is shaped like a ball. It is impossible to see all of the ball from one view. To see it all, we must flatten it out first (see page 5).

Also, because things on Earth's surface have been made smaller (using scale), they cannot be shown as they really are. So people who make maps use symbols (see page 9). Symbols are simple shapes and colors that stand for something in the real world, such as a capital city, a mountain range, an apple farm, or your school.

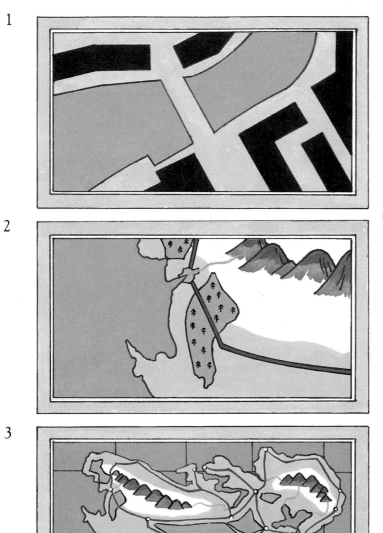

1

2

3

Map 1 is a close-up of map 2, showing the area around the bridge in detail. Map 3 uses a much smaller scale. In the same area on the page, it shows the entire island.

Making the Earth flat

The whole surface of a ball cannot be shown on a flat sheet of paper without cutting and stretching the ball. This is what we have to do to show the surface of Earth as a map.

If we pretend that Earth is an orange, we can divide it into segments. Even though the segments are not flat, we can now see the whole surface of the orange at once if we lay the segments out. Before we cut the orange, let's put a sticky label around it. This label will help us understand how a round shape becomes distorted when it is flattened out.

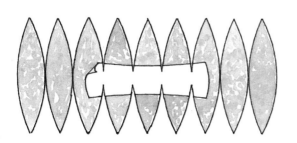

Look what has happened to the label. To get rid of the cuts or gaps, and to bring the cut parts back together, we have to stretch the pieces so they touch one another, like this:

We could lay the segments in another pattern, like this:

Or we could arrange to have a special sticky label made in this shape:

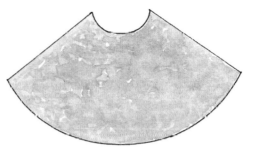

Whatever way we arrange the segments, we cannot show them as they are on the surface of a round object. We have to distort them to make them flat. This means that in making maps, we have to accept the fact that we will change distances and directions slightly.

The following pictures show how the shape of Australia can be changed by stretching it flat in different ways. Compare these maps with the map of Australia on page 41. The different ways of stretching are called projections.

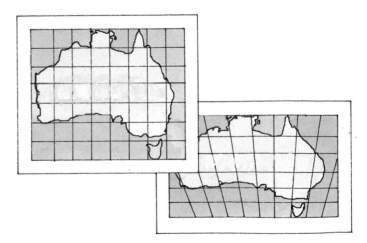

Finding the direction

Maps have a language you can learn. Their language begins with the four basic directions: north, south, east, and west. These directions answer the question, "Which way?"

North is the direction toward the North Pole from any place on Earth. South is toward the South Pole, in the opposite direction. As we face north, the direction to the right is called east. This is where the Sun appears every morning. The direction to the left as we face north is called west.

North is usually at the top of a map. If we want to find out which direction north is, we use a compass. The needle of the compass always points to north. And once we know which direction north is, we can figure out the other directions.

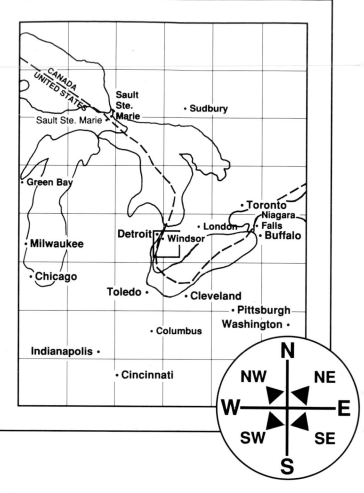

This map shows how we can use the points of a compass to divide up the continent of Africa.

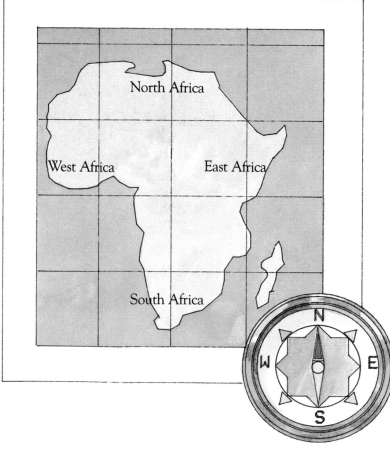

Using a compass, can you figure out in which direction you must travel from Detroit or Windsor to get to the other places marked on the map?

We can also describe other directions, too. Halfway between north and east is a direction called northeast. Halfway between east and south is called southeast.

Direction and distance can be used to describe the position of a place. For example, you could describe a city as being 100 miles (160 km) east of where you are. But we can also divide up areas, countries, and continents according to their compass position. For example, we talk about South Africa, which is a country in Africa, or East Africa, West Africa, and North Africa, which are regions that are made up of many countries.

Knowing where we are

Every place in the world has a particular position where it can always be found. You can find buildings and people by using their addresses. You have an address where letters are delivered. But what is the "address" of a city, a mountain, a forest, or an entire country?

Look at the picture below. It shows a city, a mountain, and a forest. It also has a grid of lines on it with numbers and letters down the side and along the top. Using these lines, we can give each of these places an address of sorts: The city is at A2, the mountain peak at B1, and the forest at C3. You can find the addresses by following the lines to their numbers and letters and putting them together.

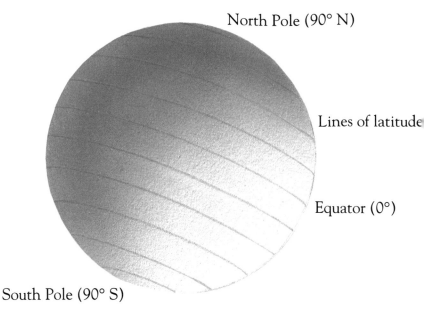

North Pole (90° N)

Lines of latitude

Equator (0°)

South Pole (90° S)

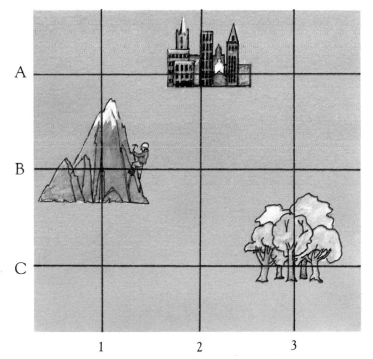

Maps use imaginary lines called lines of latitude and longitude to divide the world. Lines of latitude are circles that are drawn around the globe. They measure how far north or south a place is. All the lines of latitude run parallel to the Equator. They are given a number (a degree, or °) north or south of the Equator. They reach a maximum of 90° north at the North Pole and 90° south at the South Pole.

Lines of longitude are imaginary lines running up and down from the North Pole to the South Pole. They measure how far east or west a place is from a point known as the Greenwich meridian in London, England. This point is longitude zero. Lines of longitude are measured up to 180° east and 180° west. They meet on the other side of the world from Greenwich, near New Zealand.

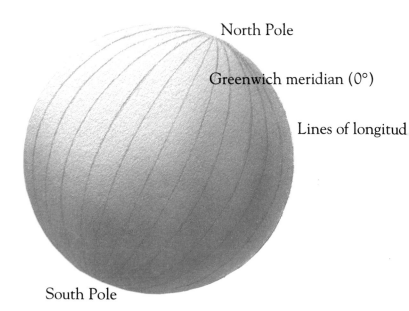

North Pole

Greenwich meridian (0°)

Lines of longitude

South Pole

How to use the scale bar

A toy car's scale is the difference in size between it and the real thing. Our toy is 32 inches (about 80 cm) long, and the real car on which it is based is 160 inches (400 cm) long. This means that 1 inch on the toy equals 5 inches on the real car. So the toy has a scale of 1:5. The real car is 5 times bigger than the toy.

A map scale is used in the same way. A scale of 1:1,000 means that if you measure a distance of 1 inch on the map, it would actually be 1,000 inches on the real ground. So scale is the system that brings things down to sizes that fit on paper. Scale lets you hold thousands of square miles on a map in your hand.

To make things easier, maps usually have a scale bar, where the measured distance and the real ground distance are matched to each other.

On each map in this atlas, the scale bar is shown as a ruler. One side shows centimeters and kilometers, and the other side shows inches and miles. The scale varies from map to map, so be careful when you measure with it!

You can measure distances on your maps by using paper. Put the edge of the paper along a line running between two points on the map. Put a mark by each point. Then put the paper on the scale bar and read off the real distance between the two points in miles or kilometers.

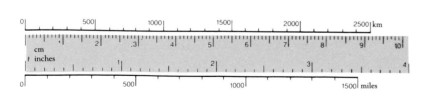

How to use the symbols

All maps use symbols. Symbols are simple images that stand for something more complicated in the real world. For example, if we want to show an area where cotton grows, we can show it by using a symbol like the one in the picture on the right. We know what a real cotton field looks like, so we can imagine it when we see the symbol on the map. But first we need to know what the symbols stand for. We can guess the meaning of some. Others may be more difficult.

Different maps use different kinds of symbols. The maps in this atlas use only a few symbols to show you some of the interesting things that go on in the world. But the world is a very complicated place, and there are many other products or activities that are not shown using our symbols.

Here are the symbols used in this atlas and their meaning, along with the meaning of the differently colored landscapes:

Cotton symbol

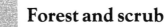
Cotton picking

♨	**Major port**
✕	**International airport**
➡	**Fishing zone**
🌾	**Cereal farming**
🍇	**Vineyards (Grapes)**
✿	**Cotton fields**
⫼	**Sugar plantations**
✳	**Cattle farming**
✿	**Sheep farming**
𝕏	**Goat herding**
⬛	**Rubber plantations**

⛟	**Coal mining**
🛢	**Oil wells**
♨	**Gas**
⛩	**Dam**
✿	**Heavy industry**
🐘	**Game reserve**
■	**Capital city**
□	**Important town or city**
△	**Mountain peak**

	Mountains
	Forest and scrub
	Desert
	Arable land
	Frozen desert (snow and ice)

9

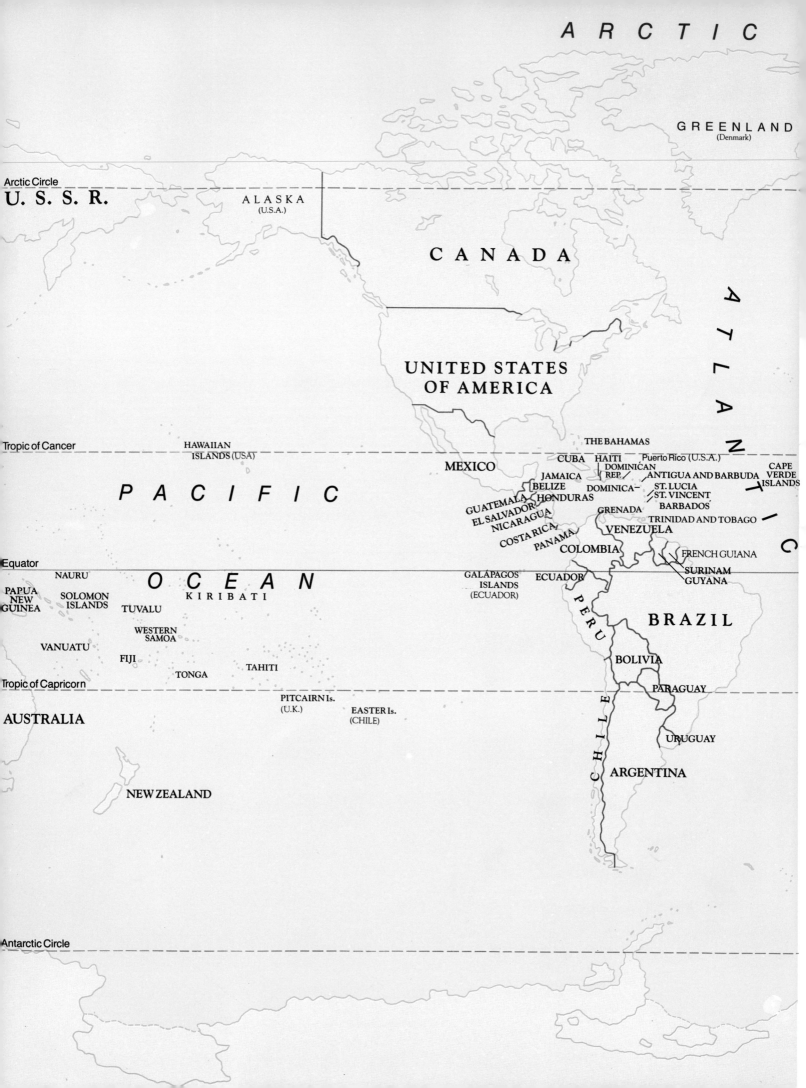

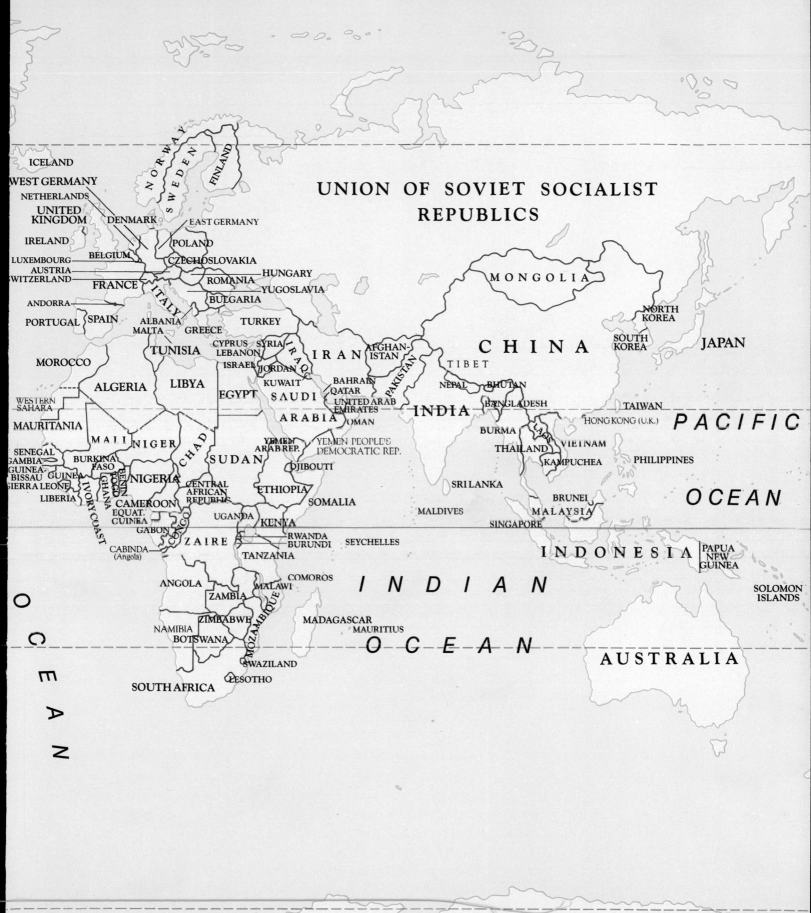

OCEAN

ICELAND
WEST GERMANY
NETHERLANDS
UNITED
KINGDOM
IRELAND
LUXEMBOURG
AUSTRIA
SWITZERLAND
ANDORRA
PORTUGAL
SPAIN
MOROCCO
WESTERN
SAHARA
MAURITANIA
SENEGAL
GAMBIA
GUINEA-
BISSAU
SIERRA LEONE
LIBERIA

NORWAY
SWEDEN
FINLAND
DENMARK
EAST GERMANY
POLAND
BELGIUM
CZECHOSLOVAKIA
FRANCE
ITALY
ROMANIA
HUNGARY
YUGOSLAVIA
BULGARIA
ALBANIA
MALTA
GREECE
TUNISIA
ALGERIA
LIBYA
TURKEY
CYPRUS
LEBANON
SYRIA
ISRAEL
JORDAN
IRAQ
EGYPT
KUWAIT
SAUDI
BAHRAIN
QATAR
UNITED ARAB
EMIRATES
ARABIA
OMAN
YEMEN
ARAB REP.
YEMEN PEOPLE'S
DEMOCRATIC REP.
DJIBOUTI
MALI
NIGER
CHAD
SUDAN
BURKINA
FASO
NIGERIA
BENIN
TOGO
GHANA
GUINEA
IVORY COAST
CAMEROON
CENTRAL
AFRICAN
REPUBLIC
ETHIOPIA
SOMALIA
EQUAT.
GUINEA
GABON
CONGO
UGANDA
KENYA
ZAIRE
RWANDA
BURUNDI
SEYCHELLES
CABINDA
(Angola)
TANZANIA

UNION OF SOVIET SOCIALIST
REPUBLICS

MONGOLIA

CHINA

NORTH
KOREA
SOUTH
KOREA
JAPAN

TIBET

AFGHAN-
ISTAN

IRAN

PAKISTAN

NEPAL
BHUTAN
BANGLADESH
TAIWAN
INDIA
BURMA
LAOS
VIETNAM
THAILAND
KAMPUCHEA
PHILIPPINES
SRI LANKA
BRUNEI
MALDIVES
MALAYSIA
SINGAPORE

PACIFIC

OCEAN

INDONESIA
PAPUA
NEW
GUINEA

SOLOMON
ISLANDS

ANGOLA
MALAWI
COMOROS
ZAMBIA
ZIMBABWE
MOZAMBIQUE
NAMIBIA
BOTSWANA
MADAGASCAR
MAURITIUS
SWAZILAND
LESOTHO
SOUTH AFRICA

INDIAN

OCEAN

AUSTRALIA

OCEAN

ANTARCTICA

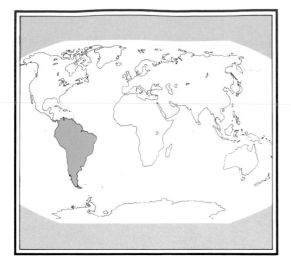

(Right) The carnival at Rio de Janeiro, Brazil. This popular religious festival takes place every year just before Lent.

Activities

- How far is it from Brasília to Buenos Aires?
- Which is the largest country in South America?
- The Equator runs through three South American countries. Which are they?
- Which six countries lie on longitude 60° W? And which islands?
- In which ocean is the mouth of the Amazon River?
- What is the capital of Venezuela?
- Mount Chimborazo is an extinct volcano in the Andes. How high is it?
- How many countries are there in South America?

Regional Facts

Population: 270 million

Largest Country: Brazil

Smallest Country: French Guiana

Largest City: São Paulo, Brazil, 7 million people

Highest Mountain: Aconcagua, Argentina, 22,831 ft (6,959 m)

Longest River: Amazon, 4,000 miles (6,440 km) — the second longest river in the world

South America

South America is a continent of very different landscapes. The Andes mountain range runs near the Pacific coast along the length of the continent. It is nearly 4,500 miles (7,250 km) long. Some of the mountains are volcanoes.

More than half of South America is covered by forests. This includes the huge Amazonian rain forest, found mainly in Brazil, the largest country. Hundreds of different types of trees grow in this forest. The Amazon River flows through it. It is one of the world's greatest rivers and has more than 1,000 small rivers running into it.

The Atacama Desert is one of the driest places on Earth. Some parts have never had any rain. The southern tip of the continent is very cold. It is not far from the harsh, frozen wastes of Antarctica.

The first people to live in South America were tribal Indians. About 400 years ago, Spanish and Portuguese people landed and started to colonize different areas. Today, most of the people in the continent's thirteen countries speak either Spanish or Portuguese. Indian languages are spoken in some parts. Most people practice the Roman Catholic religion, brought over from Europe.

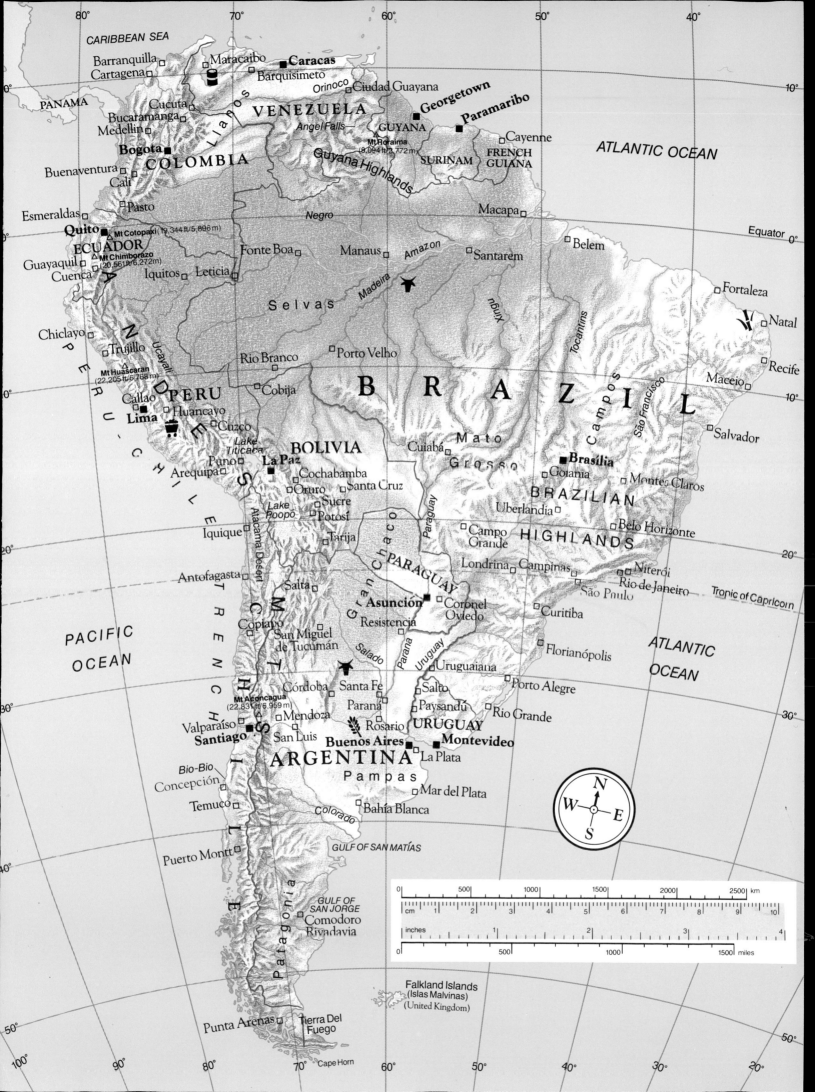

Central America, Mexico, and the Caribbean

Working on a sugar plantation.

Actually part of North America, Mexico is the largest country in this region. It is almost four times bigger than the seven countries of Central America put together. At the southern end of Central America, the Caribbean Sea is joined to the Pacific Ocean by the Panama Canal.

Most of the people of this area are a mixture of Indians who first lived here and Europeans who came to find gold. More than half are mestizos, a mixture of American Indian and European ancestry. The European colonizers brought in Christianity, but in some areas traditional Indian religions are still practiced.

In the Caribbean Sea there is a group of islands that stretches in a crescent shape from Florida to Venezuela in South America. Cuba is the largest island, and nearly half of all Caribbean island people live in Cuba and Haiti.

The people of the Caribbean come from many different ethnic backgrounds. Many are descended from slaves brought from Africa to work on sugar plantations. The islands have a warm, tropical climate that is very popular with vacationers from other countries. Most people work on farms or in hotels, shops, and small factories. Fruit, sugar cane, cotton, and coffee are grown, and much is sold to other countries.

Regional Facts

Population: 110 million

Largest Country: Mexico

Smallest Country: Bermuda

Largest City: Mexico City, Mexico, 14 million people

Highest Mountain: Citlaltepetl, Mexico, 18,701 ft (5,700 m)

Longest River: Rio Grande, 1,760 miles (2,832 km)

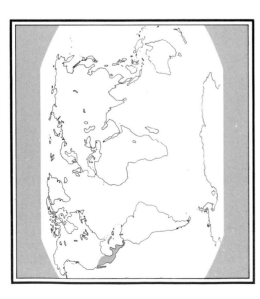

Activities

- What is the capital of Honduras?
- How far is it from Tijuana to Monterrey?
- How many countries are there in Central America?
- In which direction do you travel from Monterrey to Mexico City?
- Which island is the largest in the Caribbean Sea?
- Which Central American country lies on latitude 10° N?
- Which ocean is to the north of the West Indies?
- Which four countries border on Guatemala?
- Which republic shares an island with Haiti?
- How high is the highest mountain in Guatemala?

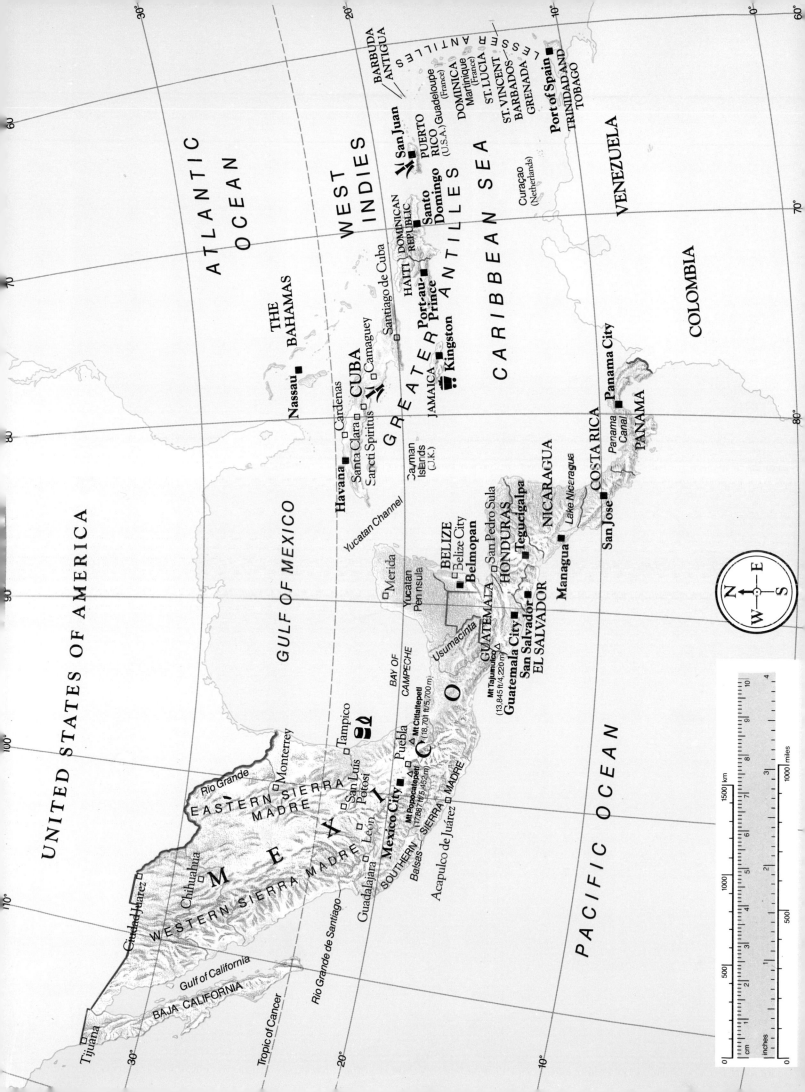

United States of America (lower forty-eight states)

The United States of America is one of the largest, richest, and most powerful countries in the world. It is made up of fifty states, several territories, and Washington, D. C. From 1912 until 1959, its flag carried forty-eight stars (one for each of the states) and thirteen stripes (for the original thirteen colonies). In January 1959, Alaska joined the United States to become the biggest state, followed by Hawaii in August 1959.

The first Europeans came to settle what is now the U.S. almost 400 years ago. They came from England and settled what became New England and Jamestown, Virginia. Others came from places like Spain and Holland, naming the places they settled after the places they had left behind. But people were already living in this land before the Europeans came. The Europeans called them Indians. There were many battles among Indians and Europeans, until the Europeans controlled almost all the land.

The U.S. is a mixture of cultures from many different nations. This has given the country a rich variety of lifestyles, food, music, and art. These have come from Indians, black Africans (brought to the U.S. as slaves), Europeans (such as Spanish, British, Dutch, Irish, Italian, and Slavic peoples), Asians, Latin Americans, and others.

Country Facts

Population: 244 million

Capital: Washington, D. C., 3 million people

Largest City: New York, 9 million people

Highest Mountain: McKinley, Alaska, 20,320 ft (6,194 m) (see pages 18 and 19)

Longest River: Missouri, 3,710 miles (5,969 km)

The U.S. is the fourth largest country in the world.

City children play baseball, a sport known as the "national pastime" by many in the United States.

Activities

- How far is it by direct flight from New Orleans to Miami?

- The smallest state lies between Massachusetts and Connecticut. What is it?

- Which ocean is to the west of the mainland United States?

- Which state is just to the east of Arizona?

- What is the highest mountain in the lower forty-eight states and what famous city is it close to?

- What is the capital of the U.S.?

- In which state is the Grand Canyon?

- On what river is the Hoover Dam?

- What are the main mountain ranges in the lower forty-eight states?

Canada, Alaska (U.S.), and Greenland

Logging on the St. Lawrence Seaway.

Canada is the second largest country in the world after the U.S.S.R. Much of Canada is very cold in winter and covered with snow. In the north is a group of large, ice-covered islands in the Arctic Ocean, where very few people live.

South of the islands are vast areas of pine forest. Most Canadians live in the country's southernmost part, near the Great Lakes and the St. Lawrence River. Part of the Canada-U.S. border runs through the lakes and the river.

To the northwest of the Great Lakes are Canada's prairies, where enormous wheat farms stretch as far as the eye can see. Farther west are the high Rocky Mountains, which stretch down into the United States.

Most of the Canadian people are of British and French descent. American Indians and Inuit (Eskimo) were the original inhabitants.

Canada is one of the world's richest countries. Wheat farming, wood, fish, oil, minerals, and gas provide great wealth for this modern nation.

Alaska is joined to Canada but is a part of the U.S. It is the largest of the states in area, but because it is mostly frozen, mountainous, and barren, few people live there.

Greenland is nearly covered by a huge ice cap, making it the world's largest ice mass outside of Antarctica. Because of its extreme climate and geography, only about 54,000 people live in Greenland, most of them a mixture of native Inuit and mainly Danish European immigrants.

Regional Facts

Population: 25 million

Capital (Canada): Ottawa, 285,000 people

Largest City: Montréal, Canada, 980,000 people

Highest Mountain: McKinley, Alaska, 20,320 ft (6,194 m)

Longest River: Mackenzie-Peace-Finlay, 2,635 miles (4,241 km)

Largest Lake: Superior, the largest freshwater lake in the world

Canada is the second largest country in the world. Greenland is the largest island in the world.

Activities

- In which province is Calgary?
- On which lake is Yellowknife?
- Which two islands lie on the Arctic Circle?
- How far is it from Winnipeg to Montréal?
- What country has authority over Greenland?
- Between which two lakes is Sault Sainte Marie?
- In which direction do you travel from Sudbury to Montréal?
- In which bay do latitude 60° N and longitude 85° W meet?

Scandinavia

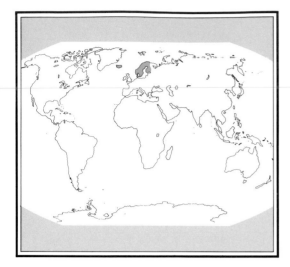

Activities

- Which Scandinavian country is farthest from the Arctic Circle?

- What is the capital of Iceland?

- In which direction do you travel from Malmö to Stockholm?

- Which Swedish town is east of Copenhagen?

- Which gulf separates Sweden and Finland?

- How far is it from Oslo to Copenhagen?

- In which ocean is Iceland?

- Approximately how far is it across Iceland from east to west?

- Which latitude touches the northern tip of Iceland?

- Which Scandinavian country has the northernmost point?

These Samit (Lapps) are herding reindeer.

Denmark, Sweden, Norway, Iceland, and Finland make up the part of Europe called Scandinavia. Denmark is made up of a peninsula called Jutland and about 500 small islands. It has some of the most productive farms in the world and exports meat and cheese to other European countries.

Sweden and Finland are beautiful countries, covered with thick forests. The paper industry in Sweden is important to the people. Huge mills turn wood from the forests into paper. Finland is peppered with lakes. There are about 60,000 in all. Norway is very mountainous, with deep fjords (see above) cut into the coastline by large glaciers in the last Ice Age. Many fishing trawlers leave the coastal towns to gather their catch of fish in the North Sea.

The northern parts of Scandinavia are sometimes called "the land of the midnight Sun." Because the land is so far north, beyond the Arctic Circle, the Sun shines all through the night for a few days each summer. In winter the opposite is true: For a few days, the Sun does not rise above the horizon. In the far north, Samit (Lapps) herd reindeer.

Iceland is just south of the Arctic Circle, in the North Atlantic. As in Norway, fishing is very important to the people who live there. The landscape is frozen and covered in parts by glaciers. Yet Iceland is home to active volcanoes and hot springs that bubble up from under Earth's surface.

Regional Facts

Population: 22.4 million

Largest Country: Sweden

Smallest Country: Denmark

Largest City: Stockholm, Sweden, 1.5 million people

Highest Mountain: Galdhoppigen, Norway, 8,103 ft (2,469 m)

Longest River: Glama, Norway, 380 miles (611 km)

ICELAND

Vatneyri

Akureyri

Reykjavik

Vatnajokull

Hofn

ATLANTIC
OCEAN

Mt Hekla
(4,747ft/1,491m)

Mt Oraefajokull
(7214 ft/2199 m)

Arctic Circle

20°

20°

BARENTS
SEA

North Cape

70°

Varanger Fjord

Alta

Tromso

Lake Inari

Vesteralen
Islands

Lapland

Narvik

Mt Kebnekaise
(6,926ft/2,111m)

Kiruna

Arctic Circle

Lofoten
Islands

Bodo

Torne

NORWEGIAN

SEA

Lulea

Oulu

U.S.S.R.

Skelleftea

Trondheim

Umea

GULF OF BOTHNIA

FINLAND

Dombas

Vaasa

Mt Galdhoppigen
(8,103ft/2,469m)

Sundsvall

Lillehammer

Lagen

Glama

Tampere

Voss

Bergen

60°

Turku

Helsinki

60°

Oslo

GULF OF FINLAND

Stavanger

Notodden

Uppsala

30°

Kristiansand

Lake
Vanern

Stockholm

Lake
Malaren

Norrkoping

Lake
Vattern

Linkoping

Skagerrak

Gothenburg

Gotland

U.S.S.R.

Boras

Alborg

Oland

Kattegat

BALTIC SEA

Jutland

Arhus

Copenhagen

Helsingborg

Esbjerg

DENMARK

Malmö

Odense

NORTH

SEA

Bornholm

EAST
GERMANY

WEST
GERMANY

10°

N

W

E

S

0   500 km

cm   1   2   3   4   5   6   7   8   9   10

inches   1   2   3   4

0   400 miles

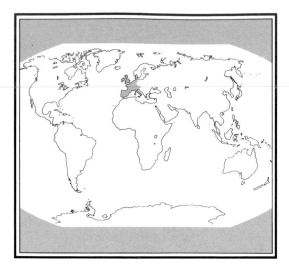

West Europe

Industry is very important to the countries of western Europe. Things made in European factories are sold all over the world. Farming is also a major business in Europe. Grapes and olives are two of the many products grown in the warm countries of the Mediterranean (Italy, France, Portugal, and Spain). Dairy produce and grain are more common in the colder, wetter countries, like Germany and Britain.

France is the largest country in Europe. It has always been popular with vacationers for its varied landscape, warm climate, good food and wine, and beautiful cities.

Switzerland and Austria are mountainous, and many people from other countries are lured to the Alps by winter skiing. The Low Countries consist of Belgium, the Netherlands, and Luxembourg. Some of the land in the Netherlands is below sea level. Great dikes have been built to keep the sea from flooding the fertile land behind them.

Spain and Portugal are also popular with tourists. Portugal is the world's leading producer of cork, which comes from the bark of a tree grown in that country. Spain was ruled by the Romans for over 600 years, and the remains of Roman buildings and walls can be seen all over the country. The Arabs also conquered parts of Spain in the Middle Ages. One of their most famous sites is the Alhambra, a palace near Granada, in southern Spain.

Activities

- Which islands lie to the east of Valencia, Spain?
- What is the longitude of London, England?
- Which three countries border on Luxembourg?
- Which river flows through Paris?
- What is the capital of Portugal?
- In which direction do you travel from Paris to Barcelona?
- Which four countries make up the United Kingdom?
- Which mountain range separates France from Spain?
- How far is it from London to Edinburgh?
- Which sea is to the east of Scotland?

Grape-picking is a common sight in countries like France, Spain, and Italy. Most of the grapes will be used to make wine.

Regional Facts

Population: 320 million

Largest Country: France

Smallest Country: Vatican City

Largest City: London, England, 6.7 million people

Highest Mountain: Mont Blanc, France, 15,771 ft (4,807 m)

Longest River: Rhine, 820 miles (1,320 km)

10° **0°** **10°** **20°** **FINLAND**

60°

Faeroe
Islands
(Denmark)

Shetland
Islands

NORWAY

SWEDEN

U.S.S.R.

Orkney
Islands

Ben Nevis
(4,406 ft/1,343 m)

SCOTLAND

DENMARK

Glasgow □ □ Edinburgh

NORTH

NORTHERN
IRELAND □ Belfast

UNITED

SEA

Hamburg □

EAST
GERMANY

POLAND

□ Galway

Dublin

KINGDOM

IRELAND

IRISH
SEA

Liverpool □ □ Manchester

NETHERLANDS

Hanover □

□ Cork

WALES

Birmingham
ENGLAND

Amsterdam
The Hague

Ijsselmeer
□ Utrecht

□ Cardiff

Thames

London

□ Rotterdam

Antwerp

□ Bristol

Southampton □

Dover
Calais

Bruges

Maastricht

Cologne

□ Plymouth

Lille

Brussels

Liège

Bonn **WEST**

50°

ENGLISH CHANNEL

BELGIUM

Frankfurt □

CZECHOSLOVAKIA

Channel
Islands
(U.K.)

LUXEMBOURG

Mannheim □ □ Nuremberg

Mosel

Luxembourg

Rhine

GERMANY

Seine

Paris

Strasbourg □

Stuttgart □

Vienna ■

□ Nantes

Loire

Dijon □

Black
Forest

VOSGES

Berne

Zurich

Munich □

Salzberg □

AUSTRIA

□ Graz

HUNGARY

ATLANTIC

SWITZERLAND

Basle □

Innsbruck □

Mt Grossglockner
(12,457 ft/3,797 m)

20°

OCEAN

Lausanne □

FRANCE

Mont Blanc
(15,771 ft/4,807 m)

LIECHTENSTEIN

□ Trieste

BAY OF BISCAY

CENTRAL

Lyon □

Mount Rosa
(15,203 ft/4,634 m)

Verona □

□ Venice

□ Bordeaux

Dordogne

MASSIF

Milan □

Po

Turin □

□ Bologna

SANMARINO

YUGOSLAVIA

Garonne

Avignon □

Genoa □

Florence □

APENNINES

CANTABRIAN MOUNTAINS

□ Bilbao

Montpellier □

Marseille □ MONACO

Pisa □

ITALY

ADRIATIC
SEA

Pico de Aneto
(11,168 ft/3,404 m)

Toulouse □

Siena □

Tiber

□ Porto

Duero

Zaragoza □

PYRENEES

ANDORRA

Corsica
(France)

VATICAN
CITY

Rome ■

□ Bari

Ebro

SPAIN

40°

Tagus

Madrid ■

Barcelona □

Naples □

Lisbon

Guadiana

Majorca

Sardinia

□ Córdoba

Guadalquivir

Granada
Mt Mulhacen
(11,411 ft/3,478 m)

Valencia

Balearic Islands

MEDITERRANEAN

Palermo □

□ Messina

□ Cádiz

Málaga □

Marsala

Sicily

Catania

Gibraltar
(United Kingdom)

SEA

ALGERIA

TUNISIA

Valletta ■ MALTA

MOROCCO

N
W — E
S

0 500 1000 km

cm 1 2 3 4 5 6 7 8 9 10

inches 1 2 3 4

0 500 miles

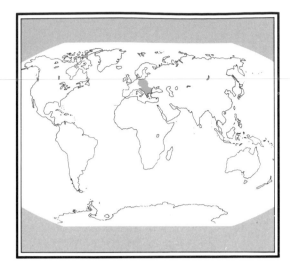

East Europe

The peoples in this part of Europe have many different customs and histories. Ancient Greek civilization and its writers and philosophers have influenced all Europe — and the Western world — with their ideas. Many ancient Greek buildings, like the Parthenon in Athens, still remain.

Yugoslavia and Greece are popular with tourists today because of their warm Mediterranean climate, their beaches, and their beautiful old towns.

Poland is the largest country in this part of Europe. It has big ports on the Baltic Sea and many large industries, and it produces a lot of coal. Czechoslovakia and Hungary do not have a coastline. They use the Danube River to carry large barges laden with goods up and down their countries. The Danube also forms part of the border between Romania and Bulgaria before it finally flows out into the Black Sea. Great cities, like Budapest, have grown up on its banks.

The countryside is a mixture of large, flat plains, where farmers grow crops and keep animals, and mountain ranges with sheltered valleys and winding rivers. Farming is very important to the livelihoods of many of the people.

Activities

- Which two countries are on the eastern edge of the Adriatic Sea?

- What is the capital of Poland?

- Which river flows through Budapest, the capital of Hungary?

- Which Greek island is farthest south?

- How far is it from Warsaw to Athens?

- In which direction do you travel to get from Belgrade to Bucharest?

- Which five countries lie on longitude 20° E?

- Into which sea does the Danube River flow?

Budapest is the capital city of Hungary. It has grown up on both banks of the Danube River.

Regional Facts

Population: 148 million

Largest Country: Poland

Smallest Country: Albania

Largest City: Athens, Greece, 3 million people

Highest Mountain: Olympus, Greece, 9,570 ft (2,917 m)

Longest River: Danube, 1,776 miles (2,858 km)

10°

DENMARK

BALTIC
SEA

20°

30°

□ Rostock

Gdańsk □

□ Szczecin

Elbe

Oder

Berlin ■

**EAST
GERMANY**

Leipzig □

Weimar □

Jena □

□ Dresden

Poznań □

Vistula

POLAND

Łódź □

□ Wrocław

Warsaw ■

U.S.S.R.

50°

**WEST
GERMANY**

ORE
MOUNTAINS

Prague ■

CZECHOSLOVAKIA

Ostrava ○

Kraków □

TATRA
MOUNTAINS

CARPATHIAN MOUNTAINS

Brno □

□ Košice

AUSTRIA

□ Bratislava

Danube

□ Miskolc

Budapest ■

□ Debrecen

HUNGARY

Lake
Balaton

Hungarian Plain

Szeged ○

Cluj □

Mureş

ROMANIA

Mt Moldoveanul
(8,348ft/2,548m) △

□ Braşov

Zagreb □

Pécs □

Arad ○

□ Timişoara

TRANSYLVANIAN ALPS

□ Ploieşti

Rijeka □

Drava

Sava

Belgrade ■

Bucharest ■

Constanţa □

ITALY

ADRIATIC
SEA

Split ○

Dubrovnik ○

D
i
n
a
r
i
c

A
L
P
S

D
a
l
m
a
t
i
a

YUGOSLAVIA

Sarajevo □

Danube

BALKAN MOUNTAINS

BULGARIA

Varna □

BLACK
SEA

Skopje □

Sofia ■

□ Stara Zagora

Burgas □

Plovdiv □

Tirana ■

ALBANIA

Vlorë □

Korçë □

□ Thessaloniki

Mt. Olympus
(9,570 ft/2,918 m) △

Corfu

Ionian Islands

PINDUS MOUNTAINS

AEGEAN
SEA

Lesbos

TURKEY

GREECE

Chios

Patrai □

Corinth □

Peloponnese

Athens ■

Rhodes

MEDITERRANEAN SEA

N
W   E
S

40°

9°

9°

500 km
cm   1   2   3   4   5   6   7   8   9   10
inches   1   2   3   4
500 miles

Crete

30°

Northern Africa

The boundaries of the vast Sahara Desert are unclear, but it is nearly as big as the U.S. and stretches across almost all of northern Africa, covering part or all of at least ten countries. Scattered across the desert are oases, where water is found. Many oases are single small springs with a few palm trees. Nomads who live in the desert bring their animals to drink there.

In the northern part of the Sahara, most people speak Arabic. In Egypt, people live along the fertile Nile Valley. The Nile is the longest river in the world, flowing all the way from central Africa to the Mediterranean Sea. Before the Aswan High Dam was completed in 1971, the Nile flooded once a year. The rich soil left by the river on both of its banks is very fertile. This has helped farmers since the time of the ancient Egyptians, who built the Pyramids and Sphinx. The Blue Nile begins in Ethiopia, one of the poorest countries in the world. Despite large amounts of foreign aid, the people have suffered widespread famine. Across the continent, in Nigeria, the situation is somewhat different. The discovery of oil has brought wealth to that country, but Nigeria still has economic problems. Most African nations were once European colonies, but today they are independent nations. Whether they are relatively rich or poor depends a lot on their natural resources and climate.

Activities

- How far is it from Algiers to Lagos?
- In which direction do you travel to get from Algiers to Lagos?
- Which four countries border on Lake Chad?
- Is the White Nile west or east of the Blue Nile?
- What is the longitude of Lake Volta, Ghana?
- What is the capital of Ethiopia?
- What is the highest point in the Atlas Mountains, Morocco?
- Which seas are connected by the Suez Canal?
- What is the quickest route by sea from Mogadiscio, Somalia, to Italy?
- Name the countries on the coast between Guinea and Nigeria.

The Aswan High Dam, on the Nile River in Egypt.

Regional Facts

Population: 293 million

Largest Country: The Sudan

Smallest Country: São Tomé and Principe (see page 29)

Largest City: Cairo, Egypt, 5 million people

Highest Mountain: Ras Dashan, Ethiopia, 15,157 ft (4,620 m)

Longest River: Nile, 4,132 miles (6,650 km) — longest river in the world

Central and Southern Africa

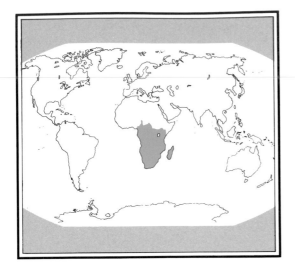

Activities

- Which African country is farthest south?
- Approximately how long is Lake Malawi?
- Which two countries share the Victoria Falls?
- In which direction do you travel from Malawi to Congo?
- How far is it between the peaks of Mount Kenya and Mount Kilimanjaro?
- What is the other, older name for the Zaire River?
- Which cape would you sail around to get from Madagascar to Namibia?
- In which countries is the Kalahari Desert?
- Which six African countries lie on the Equator?

Regional Facts

Population: 176 million

Largest Country: Zaire

Smallest Country: Seychelles (islands; not on map)

Largest City: Johannesburg, South Africa, 1.4 million people

Highest Mountain: Kilimanjaro, Tanzania, 19,340 ft (5,895 m)

Longest River: Zaire, 2,718 miles (4,374 km)

Largest Lake: Victoria — the second largest freshwater lake in the world

Countries like Kenya and Tanzania are famous for their wildlife parks.

Much of central Africa is covered by savanna, flat grassland with patches of trees and scrub. This is the home of the last great herds of wild animals — lions, giraffes, zebras, elephants, and many others. The nations of eastern Africa, such as Kenya and Tanzania, are famous for their wildlife. People can go on safari and see animals roaming in the wild.

At the heart of southern Africa is the Kalahari Desert, where native tribes still live in their traditional way. Often, women collect nuts and berries to eat, and men hunt animals with bows and poisoned arrows.

There are many different black African peoples, from the smallest people in the world, the Pygmies of the rain forests, to the tall Masai of the savanna. Many whites of European descent live in the Republic of South Africa. Though most people living there are black, whites govern this country under apartheid, a cruel system that keeps nonwhites from enjoying the same rights as whites have. Most black Africans in South Africa are from four major groups: the Nguni, the Sotho, the San, and the Khoikhoi.

10° 0°

N
W · E
S

CHAD

SUDAN

ETHIOPIA

Lake Chad

NIGERIA

ADAMAQUA MOUNTAINS

CENTRAL AFRICAN
REPUBLIC

SOMALIA

Mount
ameroon
53ft/4,070m) △

CAMEROON

□ Douala

■ Bangui

Uele

White Nile

*Lake
Turkana*

■ **Yaounde**

■ **Malabo**

Zaire

ULF
OF
EQUATORIAL
GUINEA
UINEA

■ **Libreville**

GABON

Kisangani
□
✕ *Boyoma Falls*

■ **Kampala**

UGANDA

Kisumu
□

KENYA

△ Mount
Kenya
(17,058ft/5,200m)

Equator

ÃO TOMÉ
AND
RINCIPE

CONGO

Congo

ZAIRE

Bukavu
□

RWANDA
■ **Kigali**

*Lake
Victoria*

Entebbe
□

■ **Nairobi**

■ **Brazzaville**

Pointe Noire
□

CABINDA
(Angola)

■ **Kinshasa**

□ Matadi

Kananga
□

Kwango

Kasai

Mouji-Mayi
□

Lualaba

*Lake
Tanganyika*

■ **Bujumbura**

BURUNDI

Mount Kilimanjaro
(19,340ft/5,895m) △

TANZANIA

Dodoma
□

□ Zanzibar

□ Mombasa

INDIAN OCEAN

■ **Dar es Salaam**

■ **Luanda**

ATLANTIC
OCEAN

Lobito
□

ANGOLA

Huambo
□

Likasi
□

Lubumbashi
□

Kitwe
□
Ndola □

*Lake
Bangweula*

*Lake
Malawi*

*Lake
Nyasa*

Ruvuma

Aldabra

■ **Moroni** COMOROS

□ Antseranana

MALAWI

ZAMBIA

■ **Lusaka**

Cubango

■ **Lilongwe**

□ Moçambique

□ Nampula

Zambezi

Kafue

Blantyre
□

MOZAMBIQUE CHANNEL

Toamasina
□

Maramba
□

*Lake
Kariba*

■ **Harare**

Mutare
□

■ **Antanonarivo**

MADAGASCAR

*Victoria
Falls*

ZIMBABWE

Gweru □

Beira
□

MOZAMBIQUE

*Okavango
Swamp*

Bulawayo
□

Francistown
□

NAMIBIA

BOTSWANA

Limpopo

Tropic of Capricorn

WALVIS BAY
(South Africa) □

Windhoek KALAHARI

DESERT

Pietersburg
□

DESERT

Namib Desert

■ **Gaborone**

Johannesburg
□

■ **Pretoria**

■ **Maputo**

■ **Mbabane**
SWAZILAND

REPUBLIC
Vaal

Welkom
□

Kimberley
□
Bloemfontein □

OF

■ **Maseru**

Pietermaritzburg
□

DRAKENSBERG MOUNTAINS

Orange

LESOTHO

Durban
□

SOUTH AFRICA

Great Karoo

□ East London

Cape Town

Cape of
Good Hope

Port Elizabeth
□

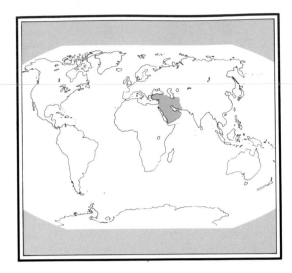

Southwest Asia

This region, which is part of the Middle East, is sometimes called "the cradle of civilization." Some of the most ancient civilizations were born here, as well as three major religions — Judaism, Christianity, and Islam. This region is also where three continents — Europe, Asia, and Africa — meet.

Most people here are Arabs, and their language is primarily Arabic. Turkey and Iran are non-Arabic nations, but like the Arabs, most people there are Muslims. Muslims believe that there is one God (Allah) and that his Prophet is Muhammad. There are Christians in Cyprus and Christians and Muslims in Israel, where most people are Jewish, and in Lebanon. The ancient Holy Land of Palestine (where Israel and Jordan are today) is sacred to Jews, Muslims, and Christians. Today, the Middle East is a scene of powerful political and religious turmoil.

Much of the Middle East is desert. It is very hot during the day and cold at night. The discovery of oil has made countries like Saudi Arabia, Bahrain, Qatar, Kuwait, and Iran wealthy. Tankers transport oil from the Persian Gulf to Europe through the Red Sea and Suez Canal.

Activities

- Which country forms the northeastern coast of the Persian Gulf?
- In which direction do you sail from Aden, Yemen, to the island of Socotra?
- Which country is north of Syria?
- What is the capital of Jordan?
- What two countries are separated by the Straits of Hormuz?
- In which country is the holy city of Mecca?
- How far is it from Mecca to Jerusalem?
- What is the longitude of Aden, Yemen?
- Which sea is close to the Elburz Mountains?
- Which Mediterranean island is in the Middle East?

Regional Facts

Population: 135 million

Largest Country: Saudi Arabia

Smallest Country: Bahrain

Largest City: Tehran, Iran, 4.5 million people

Highest Mountain: Damavand, Iran, 18,376 ft (5,601 m)

Longest River: Euphrates, 1,700 miles (2,736 km)

Oil tankers travel through the Red Sea and Suez Canal with their cargo of oil.

Union of Soviet Socialist Republics

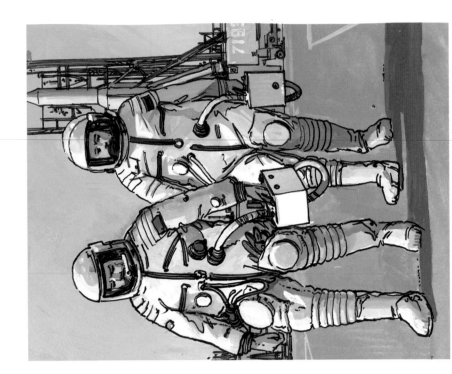

The U.S.S.R. (Soviet Union) is the largest nation in the world. It is made up of fifteen states called republics. The biggest republic is the Russian Soviet Federated Socialist Republic, with over half the population of the entire country. That is why the U.S.S.R. is often called Russia. More than sixty languages are used throughout the country, but Russian is the only language spoken everywhere.

Soviets are district councils, and the country is run through these by a system of government control and ownership called communism. Property is owned by the community, and each citizen is expected to work for the benefit of the community according to his or her abilities. A quarter of the Soviet Union is farmland, and many farmers work on enormous state-owned farms. Others work on small collectives, sharing profits with each other and the state. The Soviet Union is the world's top producer of barley, potatoes, wheat, milk, and butter.

The U.S.S.R. is also a powerful industrial nation. It has vast resources of coal, oil, and natural gas, and is the world's leading producer of steel and petroleum.

The U.S.S.R. has great military strength. With the United States and China, it is one of the world's three biggest superpowers. It also has an extensive space program. Both the first man and the first woman in space were Soviets.

Country Facts

Population: 262.5 million

Capital City: Moscow

Largest City: Moscow, 8 million people

Highest Mountain: Pik Kommunizma, 24,590 ft (7,495 m)

Longest River: Ob-Irtysh, 3,362 miles (5,411 km)

The Soviet Union is the largest country in the world.

Activities

- On which sea is Baku?

- Can you find the Black Sea and the White Sea?

- How far is it from Odessa to Leningrad?

- How many degrees of longitude does the Soviet Union extend from west to east?

- In which direction do you travel to get from Moscow to Leningrad?

- Between which two seas are the Caucasus Mountains?

- Which city is farthest west — Kiev, Moscow, or Leningrad?

- Which ocean is to the north of the Soviet Union?

- Is the U.S.S.R. twice as big as China?

- Which plateau is above the Arctic Circle?

(Above right) *The U.S.S.R. has an extensive space program.*

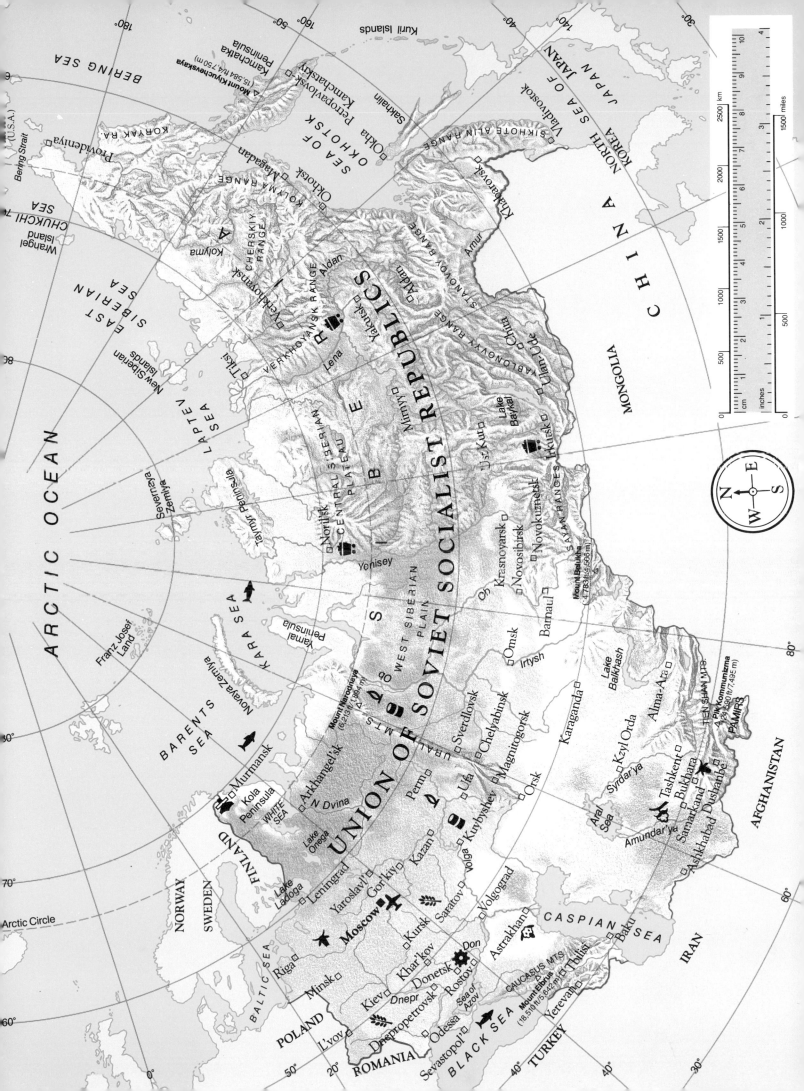

India and its neighbors

This part of the world is one of great contrasts in scenery. Northern India, Afghanistan, Bhutan, Pakistan, and Nepal are very mountainous. The highest mountain range in the world, the Himalayas, forms a spectacular border between Tibetan China and Nepal and Bhutan.

India, Pakistan, and Bangladesh are densely populated countries. India alone has 684 million people. Most live in villages and work on the land growing food. It is difficult for these nations to grow enough to feed all their people.

Most of the rain needed to grow crops falls in just a few weeks of the year. This is called the monsoon. Too much rain means floods; too little, and there will be drought.

Many different religious groups inhabit this region. Among them are Hindus, Muslims (especially in Pakistan and Bangladesh), Parsis (in Bombay), Christians, Sikhs, Buddhists, and many others.

Regional Facts

Population: 933 million

Largest Country: India

Smallest Country: Maldives

Largest City: Calcutta, India, 7 million people

Highest Mountain: Everest, Nepal/Tibetan China, 29,028 ft (8,848 m) — the highest mountain in the world

Longest River: Indus, 1,800 miles (2,900 km)

India has many large and crowded cities. This is Calcutta, in northeast India.

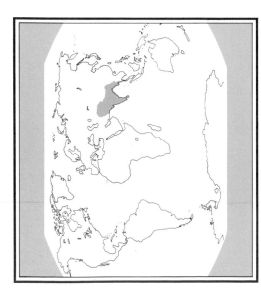

Activities

- What is the capital of Sri Lanka?
- Into which bay does the Ganges River flow?
- The second highest mountain in the world is in Pakistan, near the Indian border. What is it called?
- How far is it from Bombay to Calcutta?
- Which country is west of the Thar Desert, India?
- In which sea is the position 25° N, 65° E?
- Which country stretches farther south, Bangladesh or Pakistan?
- In which country is Kathmandu?
- To which country do the Andaman Islands belong?

China, Japan, and their neighbors

The Great Wall of China.

China is the world's third largest country. It is also the world's most populated country. A main part of the people's diet is rice, which is grown in flooded fields in southern and central China. In the cooler, drier areas of the north and east, farmers grow wheat and corn. China is the world's top producer of cotton and tobacco. While most people work as farmers, today many people in the cities work in modern factories.

Over its long history, China has often been closed to outsiders. Today, tourists visit the Great Wall, which dates back some 2,200 years and is about 1,500 miles (2,400 km) long.

Japan is the richest country in Asia. It has many successful industries that sell their products all over the world. Since World War II, Japan has become a world leader in producing calculators, cars, typewriters, pianos, and ships.

Japan is made up of four big islands (Hokkaido, Honshu, Shikoku, and Kyushu) and about 3,000 smaller ones. About fifty of Japan's mountains are active volcanoes. Fujiyama is the highest.

Regional Facts

Population: 1.15 billion

Largest Country: China — the third largest in the world

Smallest Country: Taiwan

Largest City: Tokyo, Japan, 11 million people

Highest Mountain: Everest, Tibetan China/Nepal, 29,028 ft (8,848 m) — the highest mountain in the world

Longest River: Chang Jiang, 3,964 miles (6,380 km) — the third longest river in the world

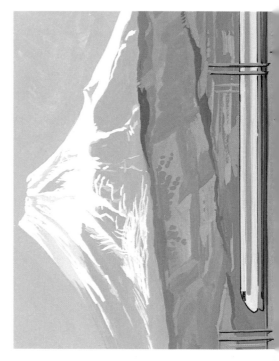

Fujiyama, a volcano, is the highest point in Japan.

Activities

- Which two countries in the world are larger than China?

- Into which sea does the Chang Jiang river flow?

- In which direction is Japan from Hong Kong?

- What is Japan's highest mountain?

- To which country does Hong Kong currently belong?

- How far is it from Shanghai to Hong Kong?

- What is the large desert in southern Mongolia and northern China called?

- What is the Chinese name for the city long called Peking?

- What is the capital of South Korea?

- Which of Japan's four large islands is farthest north?

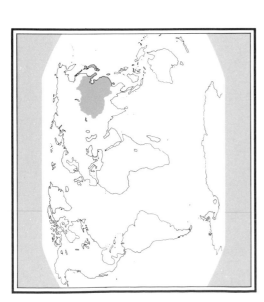

Southeast Asia

People at work on terraced rice fields.

Much of Southeast Asia is made up of islands. Indonesia has over 13,000 islands, and the Philippines has more than 7,000. Many are volcanic. This region is hot and wet all year round. For a few months each year there is a heavy rain season, called the monsoon.

Many people live in Southeast Asia. The cities are overcrowded, with poor people living on the city edges in shanty towns. Their homes are made of scrap wood and corrugated iron. Most people live on low land near the coasts and in river valleys. Many farm the land, growing rice, vegetables, spices, and fruit. Rice is a major food in this region. It is often grown on flat terraces on the sides of hills and mountains.

The many mountains are covered with thick rain forests. Some of the wood from the trees, such as teak and mahogany, is valuable. Some trees provide useful materials other than wood. The sap from the rubber tree, for example, gives us rubber. Malaysia, Indonesia, and Thailand are the world's top rubber producers. Malaysia alone produces over half the world's natural rubber. It also produces one-third of the world's tin.

Vietnam, Laos, and Kampuchea (Cambodia) are poor countries. They have suffered greatly in recent years from war and political changes.

Music, dance, plays, and handmade crafts keep alive the ancient legends of Southeast Asia. Most of the people are Buddhists or Muslims. Temple dancers tell the stories of their religion as they dance.

Regional Facts

Population: 320 million
Largest Country: Indonesia
Smallest Country: Singapore
Largest City: Jakarta, Indonesia, 6.5 million people
Highest Mountain: Jaya, Indonesia, 16,502 ft (5,030 m)
Longest River: Mekong, 2,610 miles (4,200 km)

Activities

- How far is it across the South China Sea from Da Nang to Manila?

- In which direction do you travel from Ho Chi Minh to Hanoi?

- What is the capital of Thailand?

- Two large and two small major Southeast Asian islands are on the Equator. Which are they?

- In which ocean are the Philippines?

- Which strait divides Malaysia from Sumatra?

- Is Bali east, west, north, or south of Java?

- Into which sea does the Mekong River flow?

- Which three countries border on Kampuchea (Cambodia)?

- To which group of islands does Halmahera belong?

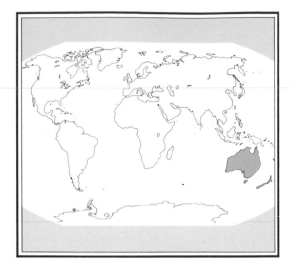

Australia and New Zealand

Australia is a country of contrasts. It has a small population, yet most of its people live in crowded cities and towns. It is the smallest continent with the greatest proportion of desert, yet one of the richest nations. It is one of the oldest land masses on Earth, yet one of the last to be developed by people. Perhaps the greatest contrast is between the Outback of vast, flat desert and sheep and cattle stations and the coastal cities where most Australians live and work. Australia also claims the distinction of being the top wool producer in the world and has many more sheep than people.

The first Australians were the Aboriginals. They have been living there for at least 40,000 years. About 200 years ago, people came from many countries in Europe, especially from Britain, and settled in what was to them a new country. They brought lifestyles with them that were quite different from the Aboriginal way of life. Major cities, like Melbourne and Sydney, look much like the cities of Europe.

The country has a varied climate. The deserts in the center are hot and dry, and the jungles in the north are hot and steamy. On the island of Tasmania, in the south, the temperature is often cool and there is plenty of rain.

The original inhabitants of New Zealand were the Maoris. They came from the Polynesian Islands, and their customs and traditions play an important role in New Zealand today. In the eighteenth and nineteenth centuries people came from Britain to start a new life farming and trading. Today, New Zealand is a rich farming country. Cattle are kept on dairy farms on North Island, and sheep graze on both islands.

Activities

- In which sea is the Great Barrier Reef?

- Which town is right in the middle of Australia?

- Which is the highest mountain in New Zealand?

- How far is it from Perth to Brisbane?

- In which direction do you travel from Sydney to Melbourne?

- In which Australian state is Brisbane?

Regional Facts

Population: Australia, 15.8 million
New Zealand, 3.3 million

Capitals: Australia, Canberra
New Zealand, Wellington

Largest City: Sydney, Australia, 3.2 million people

Highest Mountain: Mount Cook, New Zealand, 12,346 ft (3,764 m)

Longest River: Murray-Darling, Australia, 2,310 miles (3,718 m)

There are more sheep than people in Australia. They provide wool and meat.

PAPUA NEW GUINEA

120°   130°   140°   150°

I N D O N E S I A

ARAFURA SEA

Torres Strait

TIMOR SEA

10°

Melville
Island

Darwin

Arnhem Land

CORAL SEA

**GULF OF
CARPENTARIA**

Cape York
Peninsula

Cairns

INDIAN
OCEAN

Wyndham

Kimberley
Plateau

Broome

**NORTHERN
TERRITORY**

Townsville

20°

Port Hedland

Dampier

Great Sandy
Desert

Macdonnell
Range

Alice Springs

QUEENSLAND

Rockhampton

Hamersley
Range

Gibson
Desert

Tropic of Capricorn

AUSTRALIA

Cooper Creek

Charleville

Toowoomba

Carnarvon

WESTERN

Ayers Rock

Simpson

Musgrave Range   Desert

Brisbane

Meekatharra

AUSTRALIA

SOUTH

Lake Eyre

Geraldton

Great Victoria Desert

AUSTRALIA

Lake Torrens

NEW SOUTH

30°

Kalgoorlie

Nullarbor Plain

Lake Gairdner

Broken
Hill

WALES

Toowoomba

Perth
Fremantle

Esperance

Port Augusta

Darling

Murray

Wagga
Wagga

Sydney
Wollongong

Albany

GREAT AUSTRALIAN BIGHT

Port Lincoln

Adelaide

Canberra
(Australian Capital Territory)

Bendigo

VICTORIA

Mount Kosciusko
(7,316 ft/2,230 m)

TASMAN
SEA

Ballarat

Melbourne

Bass Strait

TASMANIA

Launceston

Hobart

170°   180°

PACIFIC
OCEAN

Auckland

Hamilton

North Island

Egmont
(8,252 ft/2,516 m)

**NEW
ZEALAND**

Wanganui

Napier

40°

Nelson

Palmerston North

Greymouth

Wellington

South Island

Mount Cook
(12,346 ft/3,764 m)

Christchurch

Timaru

Dunedin

Invercargill

N
W   E
S

0   500   1000   1500 km

cm 1 2 3 4 5 6 7 8 9 10

inches 1 2 3 4

0   500   1000 miles

10°

20°

30°

40°

130°   140°   150°   170°

Hawaii (U.S.) and the Pacific islands

Fishing is an important economic activity — and a way of life — on many of the Pacific islands. People still use canoes to venture out to sea to find fish.

Activities

- What is the capital of Tuvalu?
- To which country does Pitcairn Island belong?
- Which continent is to the east of the Galápagos Islands?
- What imaginary line from west to east divides the Pacific Ocean in two?
- Which two countries are separated by the Tasman Sea?
- Which country controls the Trust Territory of the Pacific Islands?
- What is the capital of Fiji?
- Which is the largest ocean on Earth?

Regional Facts

Population: 6 million

Largest Country: Papua New Guinea

Smallest Country: Nauru

Highest Mountain: Mt. Wilhelm, Papua New Guinea (not on map), 15,400 ft (4,694 m)

There are thousands of small islands in the Pacific Ocean. The ocean itself covers almost a third of the Earth's surface. The Pacific Islands fall into three main groups, according to their location and the type of people who live on them. The people of Melanesia tend to be much like the native peoples of Africa and Australia. Native Hawaiians and other people of Polynesia are related to Asian peoples. The people of Micronesia represent a mixture of the other two peoples.

Some of the islands are made of coral, the limestone skeletons of tiny sea animals. Many of these islands are quite mountainous and were created by volcanoes. The major islands of Hawaii are volcanic.

Hawaii, Fiji, and other island groups are popular with tourists, but many of the smaller islands get few visitors. Life on these islands is often simple. People live in small villages, grow food in gardens, and fish from canoes. On larger islands, people work in places like banana or pineapple plantations or mine copper and other minerals.

Some groups of islands are still colonies and belong to other countries. Others are independent, with their own governments. Hawaii became one of the fifty states of the U.S. in 1959.

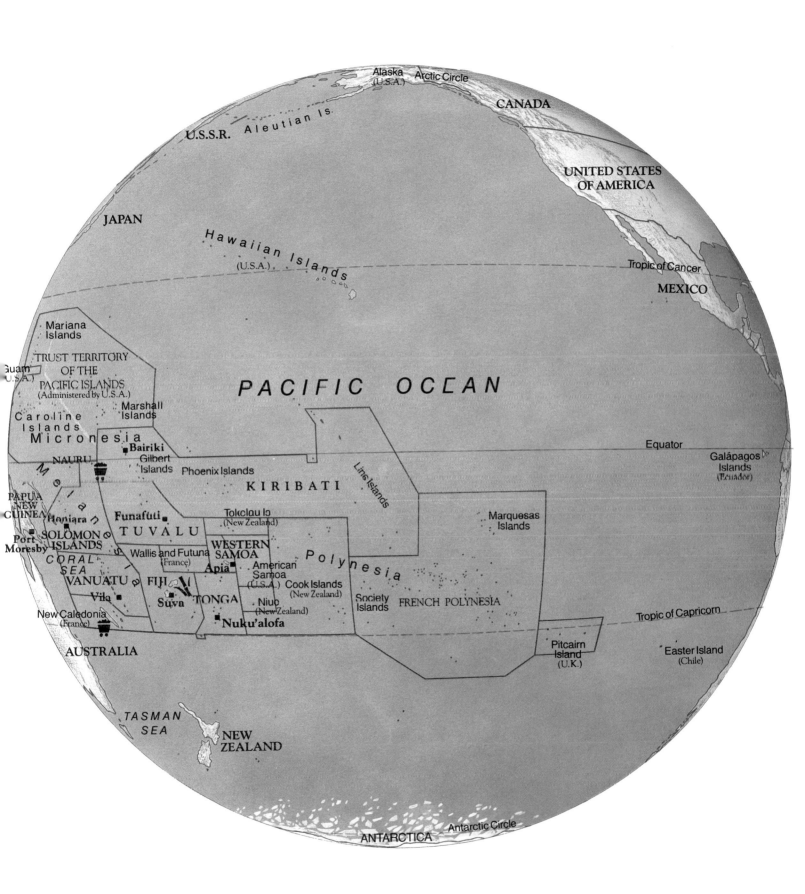

Alaska
(U.S.A.) Arctic Circle

CANADA

U.S.S.R. Aleutian Is.

UNITED STATES
OF AMERICA

JAPAN

Hawaiian Islands
(U.S.A.)

Tropic of Cancer

MEXICO

Mariana
Islands

TRUST TERRITORY
OF THE
PACIFIC ISLANDS
(Administered by U.S.A.)

PACIFIC OCEAN

Guam
(U.S.A.)

Caroline
Islands
Micronesia

Marshall
Islands

Equator

Galápagos
Islands
(Ecuador)

Bairiki
Gilbert
Islands

NAURU

Phoenix Islands

Line Islands

KIRIBATI

PAPUA
NEW
GUINEA

Honiara

Funafuti

Tokelau Is.
(New Zealand)

Marquesas
Islands

Port
Moresby

SOLOMON
ISLANDS

TUVALU

WESTERN
SAMOA

Wallis and Futuna
(France)

P o l y n e s i a

CORAL
SEA

Apia

American
Samoa
(U.S.A.)

VANUATU

FIJI

Cook Islands
(New Zealand)

FRENCH POLYNESIA

Vila

Suva

TONGA

Niue
(New Zealand)

Society
Islands

New Caledonia
(France)

Nuku'alofa

Tropic of Capricorn

AUSTRALIA

Pitcairn
Island
(U.K.)

Easter Island
(Chile)

TASMAN
SEA

NEW
ZEALAND

Antarctic Circle

ANTARCTICA

PACIFIC OCEAN

Aleutian Is.

BERING SEA

150°

180°

150°

ALASKA
(U.S.A.)

Yukon

Bering Strait

Wrangel Island

S I B E R I A

120°

Mackenzie

Inuvik

Barrow

Prudhoe Bay

BEAUFORT SEA

EAST SIBERIA SEA

New Siberian Islands

Tiksi

Lena

120°

CANADA

Banks Island

Victoria Island

LAPTEV SEA

ARCTIC OCEAN

Severnaya Zemlya

U.S.S.R.

North Pole

Noril'sk

LOMONOSOV RIDGE

Ellesmere Island

Yenisei

Ob

Franz Josef Land (U.S.S.R.)

Thule

Baffin Island

BAFFIN BAY

Novaya Zemlya

KARA SEA

Svalbard (Norway)

Davis Strait

BARENTS SEA

60°

GREENLAND (Denmark)

GREENLAND SEA

Murmansk

60°

NORWEGIAN SEA

Arkhangel'sk

ATLANTIC OCEAN

Denmark Strait

Narvik

NORWAY

SWEDEN

FINLAND

Arctic Circle

ICELAND

30°

0   500   1000   1500   2000 km

cm   1   2   3   4   5   6   7

inches   1   2   3

0   500   1000   1500 miles

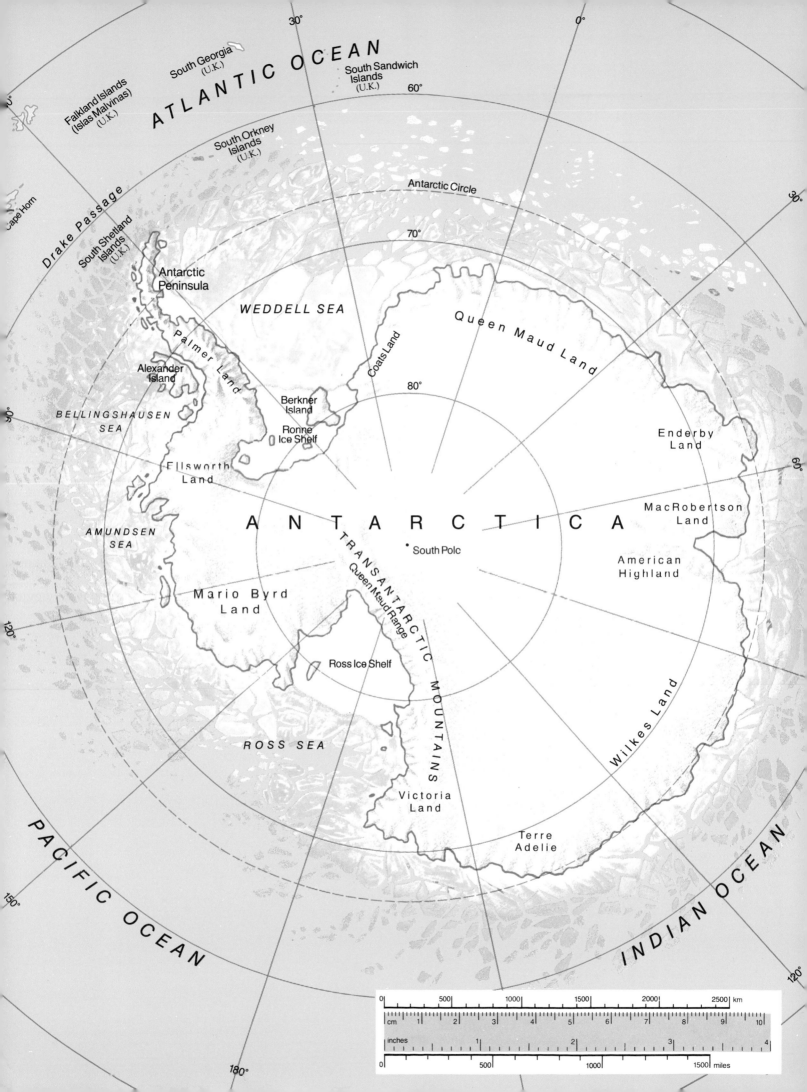

ATLANTIC OCEAN

South Georgia
(U.K.)

South Sandwich
Islands
(U.K.)

Falkland Islands
(Islas Malvinas)
(U.K.)

South Orkney
Islands
(U.K.)

Cape Horn

Antarctic Circle

Drake Passage

South Shetland
Islands (U.K.)

70°

Antarctic
Peninsula

WEDDELL SEA

Queen Maud Land

Palmer Land

Coats Land

80°

Alexander
Island

Berkner
Island

BELLINGSHAUSEN
SEA

Ronne
Ice Shelf

Enderby
Land

Ellsworth
Land

ANTARCTICA

MacRobertson
Land

AMUNDSEN
SEA

South Pole

American
Highland

Mario Byrd
Land

TRANSANTARCTIC MOUNTAINS

Queen Maud Range

Ross Ice Shelf

Wilkes Land

ROSS SEA

Victoria
Land

Terre
Adelie

PACIFIC OCEAN

INDIAN OCEAN

180°

150°

120°

| 0 | 500 | 1000 | 1500 | 2000 | 2500 km |

| cm | 1 | 2 | 3 | 4 | 5 | 6 | 7 | 8 | 9 | 10 |

| inches | | 1 | | 2 | | 3 | | 4 |

| 0 | | 500 | | 1000 | | 1500 miles |

Map Index

47

48

CLARK MEDIA CENTER